THE ART OF TEACHING & The Threat of MOOCs

by John C. Wilhelmsson

Copyright © 2014 by
John C. Wilhelmsson
All rights reserved.
ISBN-10: 0990723100
ISBN-13: 978-0990723103

The Art of Teaching

The Art of Teaching

DEDICATION

To my colleagues at San Jose State University. Never before have I been more proud to be a philosopher, or a Spartan, then when we stood together at our Thermopylae against the opportunist politicians and the greedy businessmen.

And to all those who devote themselves to the art of teaching.

The Art of Teaching

The Art of Teaching

Chaos To Order Publishing
Campbell, California

The Art of Teaching

CONTENTS

Dedication	v
Introduction	1
The Art of Teaching	9
MOOCs Defined	47
MOOCs and Academic Freedom	59
Mooctruth.com	85
Faith, Reason, and Education	103

The Art of Teaching

❋ ❋ ❋

The Art of Teaching

The Art of Teaching

INTRODUCTION

Some come to compete for prizes,
Some come to sell their wares,
But the best come as spectators.
Similarly in life,
Some grow up with servile natures,
Greedy for fame and gain,
But the philosopher seeks for truth.

Pythagoras' quote about the ancient Olympic games points out that there are three basic ways of life a person may choose: to be the one who seeks honors, to be the one who seeks profit, or to be the one who seeks truth. The critical question being: "In which of these three basic ways of life might we wish our educators to be?"

Although this might seem like a rather simple question, the facts are that our schools have recently come under a great deal of pressure from both those who seek for fame (in the form of

The Art of Teaching

opportunist politicians) and those who seek for gain (in the form of greedy businessmen). Here I am speaking of the recent attempts to force Massive Open Online Courses (MOOCs) upon our universities.

At a press conference at San Jose State University (SJSU) on April 10, 2013 Lieutenant Governor Gavin Newsom warmed up the crowd by talking about his 3 year old daughter's aptitude for the iPad (a rather ironic start to speech on technology and education given the recent revelation that former Apple CEO Steve Jobs would not let his young children near the iPad!). Newsom went on to speak of the utility of MOOCs, the overall purpose of the press conference being to announce a "*collaboration*" between MOOC supplier EdX and SJSU.

The Art of Teaching

The SJSU Philosophy Department, apparently understanding the term *"collaborator"* as "a person who cooperates traitorously with an enemy" rather than as "a person who works jointly on an activity or project" (of which it may mean either) then did something rather extraordinary. They published an open letter to Harvard University professor Michael Sandel of whose EdX MOOC, "JusticeX," the SJSU administration was attempting to force upon them.

The letter was extraordinary for two reasons. First, for the fact that an entire group of quite diverse in background and thought philosophers unanimously agreed upon it (thus answering the age old question; "Do philosophers agree upon anything?). And second, for what the letter actually said.

The Art of Teaching

The MOOC that the SJSU administration was attempting to force upon the Philosophy Department was, ironically, on the topic of social justice. And the Philosophy Department's open letter was quick to make light of this:

> *There is no pedagogical problem in our department that JusticeX solves, nor do we have a shortage of faculty capable of teaching our equivalent course. We believe that long-term financial considerations motivate the call for massively open online courses (MOOCs) at public universities such as ours. Unfortunately, the move to MOOCs comes at great peril to our university. We regard such courses as a serious compromise of quality of education and, ironically for a social justice course, a case of social injustice.*

The open letter was quickly published in a New York Times article and then

The Art of Teaching

went "viral" in the educational media around the country and, in fact, around the world!

So just as a small force of Spartans had held back the tide of the Persian hordes at Thermopylae, the SJSU Philosophy Department's open letter held back the tide of opportunist politicians and greedy businessmen who were attempting to take over public higher education. And the victory at SJSU could have been total except for the unfortunate, yet perhaps inevitable, choice of some to reenact the role of Ephialtes.

As a member of the SJSU Philosophy Department, the incident made me think more deeply about the nature of teaching. I was already writing a blog on the art of teaching so had a ready place to collect my

The Art of Teaching

thoughts. I then wrote an essay on the definition of a MOOC, showing the essential differences between MOOCs and small online courses, and I also wrote comments on the various MOOC articles of the day.

The basic reflection being upon the question: "Why is it so important for education to be done in a classroom where people are physically present together?" An early answer to this question came, ironically, from the world of high-tech itself in the form of Yahoo CEO Marissa Meyer's memo to her employees which reads in part:

> *To become the absolute best place to work, communication and collaboration will be important, so we need to be working side-by-side. That is why it is critical that we are all present in our offices.*

The Art of Teaching

And, although I do not think of the classroom as a place of work, I do think of it as a place of *"communication and collaboration"* (in the positive sense).

This book is a reflection on education which begins with the essay "The Art of Teaching" and then goes on to examine the threat of MOOCs to said art. It then looks at the issues of faith, reason, and education through the essay "A Tale of Two Traditions."

My hope here is certainly not to be comprehensive, yet rather to present a book which might allow the reader to become more informed on the issue in general and thus enrich their own reflections on the art of teaching and the threat of MOOCs.

The Art of Teaching

THE ART OF TEACHING

The Art of Teaching

The Art of Teaching

CHAPTER ONE

THE CALL OF TEACHING

Sometimes people ask me what it is like to be a university professor. In reality, at least for me, it is not that unlike any other kind of teaching. I began my teaching career as a catechist many years ago. In those days, the topics were, of course, more theological in nature yet the basic processes and principles of teaching were not unlike they are today.

Still today I consider teaching to be a "calling" rather than a "job." The first time I taught in a classroom setting was at my home parish of St. Frances Cabrini. I had volunteered to be an emergency fill-in religious education teacher but, as it turned out, the teacher of the 7th grade class could no longer

The Art of Teaching

fulfill their duties, so the task was appointed to me.

I had taught in small youth groups before where most of the people in the room were already my friends. This had been some good early experience, yet going into a classroom full of people you do not know in advance is much different. There are all these questions and fears that come upon you: Will they listen to me? If they do listen to me, will I have something interesting to say? What if someone challenges what I have to say?

These thoughts are what I like to call the "fear factor" of teaching. Many people do not realize that it can be a plain old scary thing to walk into a university lecture hall, with anywhere from 50 to 150 students in it, and try to capture their attention for an hour or

The Art of Teaching

two. A certain confidence is needed, and different people find their confidence in different ways.

Some develop, or perhaps over-develop, their ego to a point where they think that all those people are actually privileged to be in the same room with them. Others rely on great content brought about through long hours of study. They do not yet have personal confidence, yet they do have great content and that gets them through.

Confidence and content are good tools to have yet I think there is something deeper that has always carried me through. Teaching to me is not as much a "skill" as it is an "art." It is not as much a "job" as it is a "calling." And somehow, deep in my heart, I knew that I had been called into that classroom full of energetic 7th

The Art of Teaching

graders. This is not to say that I was lacking in confidence or content, yet what I had more was a deep desire to share what I had learned with others.

A "calling" is like this. It does not just all of the sudden appear one day but, instead, in a way seems to have been there all along. It is like God plants a desire in your heart and you come to understand said desire more and more over the path of your lifetime. And if you have been given a call then you know, through faith, that you have also been given a gift. Because God never calls a person to a task that they have not, in some way, been gifted for.

However, realizing such gifts is hardly something one can do on their own. I was blessed to have an old friend of the family who had known me

The Art of Teaching

since childhood as my Director of Religious Education. Barbara was a lady who was truly gifted as both an administrator and teacher. Plus, she was just plain old wise. We would often sit and talk about teaching, and she would share with me various little tidbits of wisdom she had gathered together over the years.

I remember the most important conversation happened one day when we were sitting and talking about teaching. She told me that she thought I had the gift of teaching because I cared. And that, in her experience, you could teach a catechist many things about content, but you could never really teach them how to care. Here lies the gift of teaching. In caring about the subject you teach and, even moreso, in caring about the students you are attempting to teach it to.

The Art of Teaching

At the time I was touched by Barbara's comments, yet I did not yet fully realize the implications of them. What Barbara was alluding to is that teaching is not just about taking a body of objective knowledge and imparting it onto a group of people in an accurate manner. Teaching has to do with actually caring about those people! And if you care about someone you wish to know them. To know who they are and how their story has unfolded.

I could handle the content side of teaching. As a matter of fact, the order and assurance of the material was what had drawn me to it in the first place. Yet real people are not often so orderly. As a matter of fact, at times just one 7th grader can be quite disorderly! (not to mention a classroom full of them). Just what in the world I had signed on for I did not yet know. As I look back on it

The Art of Teaching

now, I realize that teaching that first 7th grade CCD class was the foundational moment of my teaching career.

The Art of Teaching

The Art of Teaching

CHAPTER TWO

THE TRUTH SHALL BE KNOWN IN THE CLASSROOM

All of us have had a "teacher" who knew their content well yet had little ability to reach their students with it. Teaching strategy is sometimes called "pedagogy." I do not love the use of this term myself as a "pedagogue" was originally a servant who followed students to school to make sure they were learning and then beat them with a stick if they were not! Yet, since the term has now become a sort of catch all phrase for everything good and clever in education, I suppose it must be dealt with.

The huge debate going on right now in pedagogy is centered around Massive Open Online Courses (MOOCs).

The Art of Teaching

MOOCs are a new form of distance education that, despite all the hype and fancy high-tech trappings, suffers from the same problems that distance education has always suffered from. Curiously, as is most always the case with supposed "new" ideas in distance education, people on the outside looking in seem to think MOOCs are a great idea while people on the inside looking out seem to know that they are a horrible one!

Yet just what exactly is going on here? Most people who have never really, in some fashion or another, taught tend to think of pedagogy in the way I thought of it before I stepped into that classroom full of 7th grade CCD students. In that they tend to think that learning is a simple matter of the transfer of information. Almost like data input but instead of from one

The Art of Teaching

computer to another from one human being to another. These are the people who think that using fancy taped lectures must be more pedagogically sound than having an actual teacher teach. Because better input must equal better output: Right?

Here we have a prime example of naive stupidity. Yet I must admit that before I met my 7th graders, I was naively stupid as well. I was not concerned about needing a fancy taped lecture because I was fairly confident that I knew the content. Yet I was every bit as naïve in terms of thinking that I could just do some sort of human-to-human data input.

I like to run track quite a bit and have become fond of the saying "The truth shall be known on the track." This means that no matter how fast I

The Art of Teaching

think I can run on a given day or how strong I think my will to run faster is, the truth about such things can only be known by actually getting out on the track. In teaching we have a similar saying. "The truth shall be known in the classroom." This is, of course, a saying with at least two meanings. Certainly, in the days before I met my 7th graders, and in all the days since then, I have always wanted to speak the truth in the classroom. Yet the kind of "truth" this saying refers to has more to do with one's ability to teach than the content of said teaching.

Those first few sessions with my 7th graders are a bit of a blur to me today. Yet, as I recall things, they were a bit of a blur at the time as well. The kids had incredible energy that made it very difficult for them to sit still and remain quiet. Before I knew it, all sorts of side

The Art of Teaching

conversations were going on and they were doing things like writing on the chalk board and getting into one another's desks. One student even flipped the light switch off and left the classroom in total darkness! Nobody seemed willing, or perhaps able, to sit still and listen to my lectures. I tried to be more stern with them, yet it did not seem to work. I could have gotten really loud, yet I did not wish to scare them, I wished to reach them.

Now that gift that my old friend Barbara had seen in me was tested. I could have lost my temper, or I could have just quit. Yet the fact was that, despite all the problems with my class, I cared about my students and wanted to reach them. And this is exactly why a good teacher must care. Because if you do not care about your students then you will not try to reach them.

The Art of Teaching

Yet my caring about my students had suddenly changed things. The more I saw that they were real people the more I realized that my original plan to just somehow transfer information into them was simply not right. First, because they were human beings and not computers so the whole data entry analogy was simply not valid. Second, and even more importantly, because they were human beings the data entry analogy was simply not morally acceptable.

My faith told me that human beings have a certain inherent dignity because we are all created in the image of God. Yet even beyond this, the fact that they were like me made me realize that things were going to be a bit more complicated than I had first imagined. For, you see, I had never really been a good student at their age either. Not

The Art of Teaching

because I was not bright, but because I rarely felt like I had a teacher who cared about me as a person and respected my freedom.

Suddenly, I realized that teaching is a two-way street. A sort of call and response. Like one of those worship songs where the girls sing one verse, and the guys sing the other. And because teaching is a two-way street, I was going to have to find a way to reach my 7th graders. To reach each one of them right where they were at! This is why caring about your students is so important. Because if you do not care about your students, you will not reach out to them. And if you do not reach out to them the call and response, the "dance," if you will, of good teaching can never really begin to take place.

The Art of Teaching

The Art of Teaching

CHAPTER THREE

THE FUNDEMENTALS OF TEACHING

There is a great deal of concern in today's world about education. Clearly something is not working, and many people are attempting to find out why.

The roads to wisdom in life are sometimes unexpected. I used to play miniature golf with my friends and got so good at it that I beat them regularly. So, one day, out of frustration I think, one of them said to me: "You may be good at miniature golf, but I bet you would not be good at real golf." I had little ability at the time to realize just how much of an effect this remark would have on my future life, because it led me to give "real golf" a try.

The Art of Teaching

Being from quite a large family, I had never really played too much organized sports as a child. Thus, all the good lessons one gets from sports about teamwork and proper technique had been somewhat lost upon me. Now golf has very little to do with teamwork yet most everything to do with technique. For if you do not grip the club properly and take a proper stance and set up position you simply will not strike the ball well.

In other words, fundamentals are everything in golf. This wisdom about golf is something I have incorporated into my wisdom about life in general. With the wisdom saying going something like this: "When your results are not good it is always wise to review the fundamentals."

Thus, perhaps the best place for us

The Art of Teaching

to start in trying to figure out what is wrong with education is to try and understand what the fundamentals of education really are.

The word "school" comes from the Greek *"schole"* which means a place for leisure. The philosopher Josef Pieper in his work <u>Scholasticism: Personalities and Problems of Medieval Philosophy</u> explains the purpose of a school.

> *That is to say, a certain space must be left within human society in which the demands of necessity and livelihood can be ignored; an area which is sheltered from the utilities and bondages of practical life. Within such an enclosure teaching and learning, in general the concern for 'nothing but the Truth' can exist unmolested.*

*<u>Scholasticism: Personalities and Problems of Medieval Philosophy</u> by Josef Pieper page 40.

The Art of Teaching

Interestingly, if one were to attempt to describe the necessary conditions for art one would arrive at quite a similar conclusion. Perhaps only modifying "nothing but the truth" to "nothing but what is good, and true, and beautiful."

In our hearts as a society, we know that schools are supposed to be sacred places set apart for a special purpose. This is why we are always so shocked when some horrible aspect of the outside world finds its way into a school. Yet, at the same time, there is a movement in society to make schools more accountable for their bottom lines. This is manifest in all the standardized testing being done in our schools today.

Here we see the utter schizophrenia of our society at work. For at the very same time that we wish to have schools

The Art of Teaching

that are sacred domains set apart from the everyday evils of practical life, we also wish to test and measure schools in order to see just how practical they are! And this has led to the poison of "outcome-based education" creeping into the sacred domain of the school.

School is a place of art rather than a place of business. If you understand this fundamental reality, then things can begin to move forward. Unfortunately, most of our opportunist politicians have little understanding of art, or its necessary conditions, and most of our greedy businessmen would love to get a cut of all the money our society spends on public education (with the recent controversy over MOOCs being a prime example of this).

We also have an opportunity now, which should not be passed up, to

The Art of Teaching

reflect upon the vocation of the school administrator. For if the school is to be a place set apart from the bondage and dangers of practical life then the purpose of a school administrator surely is to be the agent who works on behalf of the school to bring this about. Yet how many supposed "school administrators" not only fail in this task but, in fact, "collaborate" (in the negative sense) with all of those in the outside world who wish to turn our schools into job training centers!

My old friend Barbara was not a "collaborator" but a "protector." She knew that teaching is an art so she made sure that she gave her teachers a sacred place where they could practice it. And I mean this not only in a physical but, also, in a psychological sense. Thus, I knew that, even with all the problems and struggles I was having

The Art of Teaching

with my 7th graders, Barbara had my back. And without this knowledge, and the positive environment it created, I would not have been able to even begin to practice the art of teaching.

The Art of Teaching

CHAPTER FOUR

THE ART OF TEACHING

Good speakers have something they call the ability to "read the room." This is something that is also important in good teaching. Since I teach exclusively in the mornings now there are some class sessions where the students seem a bit low on energy. On a good day, I react to their low energy by bringing some high energy of my own. I speak a little louder and pace my lecture a little faster. This is a basic example of "reading the room" as a teacher. Yet a necessary condition for this is knowing your audience well. For I cannot know if my students are low on energy unless I know what their normal level of energy is. This is what makes doing one-time special lectures much harder than teaching a university course.

The Art of Teaching

Therefore, the first thing a good teacher must do is to invest some time in getting to know his or her students. These days class sizes are so large that some special strategies are needed. I originally used the technique of 3 x 5 cards. I borrowed this technique from a fellow SJSU philosophy instructor, Brenda, who was also a graduate of St. Frances Cabrini School. You ask the students to provide a small picture and write a few facts about themselves on the 3 x 5 card. Then you invest some time and study these cards (almost like flash cards). I also have my students answer a rhetorical question about the class subject matter on the back of the card. This is a great way to get to know your students and a great way to get feedback about what material to include in the particular course.

The Art of Teaching

An issue in today's world of high-tech gadgets is that oftentimes students are so "connected" to their favorite social media website that they fail to connect with one another. Thus, the term "Phone Zombies" has become popular. I discovered this problem when a student who had just missed a class came to me asking what I had just taught? I told him that I could, given the limited time, only give him a short explanation and that his best course of action would be to ask a friend in class for their notes. Then, he wandered away silently with a lost look on his face. After this happened over and over again with many different students, I realized that they most likely did not really have any friends in class. This shocked me because I loved being a student and always had lots of friends in class. Since then, I have begun having students introduce themselves to

The Art of Teaching

one another on the first day of class. I also ask them to be sure to get some contact information as well. Many of the educational platforms, like Canvas, also have direct communication functions. Yet I found that most students did not even bother to put up a picture and a paragraph on their Canvas profiles, so I have decided to encourage them to do so by making it an official course assignment.

There were about 15 students in my CCD class so getting to know their names was not a huge problem. Seventh graders are good with things like names yet are not usually very good at describing themselves, so I relied upon my own observations and conversations with them instead. I cannot overstate the importance of these observations. For without being attentive to my students and carefully

The Art of Teaching

observing them I would not have had the knowledge I needed to practice the art of teaching.

The first thing that I noticed was that my students, rather than being low energy, were actually quite high energy (and this despite the fact that it was an evening class). However, this was a good thing because in the classroom, as in life in general, energy can be a very positive thing if one can learn how to direct it well. I also noticed that the energy of the girls was particularly directed toward the chalk board. They just loved to draw pictures on the chalk board, and they were obviously concerned about making these pictures look quite aesthetically pleasing.

Now if you know anything about 7th grade boys, or boys from 7 to 70 for that matter, you know that despite

The Art of Teaching

how detached they might act they are in fact all really concerned about how the opposite sex perceives them. Thus, the first rule of motivating the boys is always to first get the girls on your side.

The next time I saw Barbara, I asked her if I could get some colored chalk. I liked to read short Bible stories and discuss them with the class. In this way the course was not just about me lecturing but about all of us having a conversation. This movement from the subjective human freedom of your students to the objective truth of the material is a very important one. For the art of teaching is always the art of teaching your students how to think, and never about telling them what to think.

Thus, the role of a good teacher is always twofold: to equip and to

The Art of Teaching

motivate. To prepare the students for the journey and then to invite them to go along on it. For true education can never begin to happen without the free movement of the student.

The next time I came to class I brought the colored chalk and showed it to the girls. They were all happy to see it and I think, even moreso, happy that I had implicitly acknowledged that their chalk board art was a good and positive thing rather than a form of bad behavior. And in that moment of a good feeling of accord between us, I asked them if they would help me to teach the class that evening by drawing pictures and creating the scenes to represent the Bible stories I was going to read. What followed was an entirely different educational experience. The girls and I went from being opponents in competing for attention to being

The Art of Teaching

collaborators (in the best sense). And once I had the girls on my side the boys quickly followed. It was such a wonderful experience that I began to think of other creative ways I might capture the attention of my students.

    I remembered how they used to turn off the classroom lights and how the classroom would then become pitch dark when it happened, and I suddenly got an idea. Why not create in some way a path for them to go down and then suddenly turn off the lights so they could no longer see to follow the path? So, I created a handout with a path on it with the fruits of the Holy Spirit (Galatians 5:22-23) dispersed along the route. Love, joy, peace, patience, kindness, gentleness and self-control were all things they wanted to have yet how could they arrive at them? Only through the light of Christ! I then

The Art of Teaching

found several Bible quotes about how Christ is the light and printed them out on small pieces of paper.

On the night of the class, I brought all these materials and secretly asked some of the girls to collaborate in the teaching that evening by reading the Bible verses about light when I asked them to. Once the entire class had gathered, I handed out the paper with the path that had the fruits of the Holy Spirit along it. Next, I asked them all to start drawing a line down the path with a pencil and, suddenly, when they were about halfway done, I turned out the lights. The shrieks and screams of the class were palpable!

As the lights came back on, the class became silent. Then, one by one, the girls began reading aloud the Bible verses about the light of Christ. What

The Art of Teaching

followed was one of the deepest and best conversations about religious faith that one could ever possibly hope to have with a group of 7th graders! It was a very natural conversation where everyone felt comfortable talking about things like faith, family, and prayer and I even learned a few things myself along the way.

As the class session drew to a close, I realized that my students and I had begun to develop a sense of trust. And that this sense of trust was going to last into the future. It was then that I realized that I had finally learned the art of teaching.

With every class since then I have tried to develop this same sense of trust with my students. Yet every class I have taught down through the years has been quite unique and different. Not

The Art of Teaching

just because they were university students and not 7th graders, for each class at the university has been quite unique and different as well. I continue to try and know and reach my students and occasionally change my strategy to respond better to their needs. Ultimately, I judge how well I have done based upon how well they do. Because, for me, the most successful class is the one in which each and every student feels so reached and respected and part of a community that they all excel to the best of their abilities.

The Art of Teaching

MASSIVE OPEN ONLINE COURSES DEFINED

The Art of Teaching

The Art of Teaching

WHAT IS A MOOC?

In order to have an intelligent discussion about a given issue one must first define their terms. The first rule in finding a definition is to locate the genus or general category a thing fits into. The next rule is to identify the essential characteristics which separate said thing from one another in that category. This is called determining the species.

This is not the first time that a new form of education has come along and been touted as being the answer to our problems. In the nineteenth century a thing called the "Correspondence Course" came along and was given similar fanfare. A Correspondence Course usually featured written lessons with tasks to do in order to show the completion of each lesson. I originally

The Art of Teaching

studied my trade of being a Locksmith in this way. I was sent a binder full of lessons and a bunch of envelopes with keys and lock parts in them. In order to show mastery of each lesson, I would perform a task on a lock or key and then send it back to the headquarters of the correspondence school.

Later, I took a graduate level theology course in much the same way. However, this time the binders full of lessons were full of lecture outlines and arrived with a special folder full of cassette tapes. After listening to the lectures, I would arrange for a responsible person in the community to proctor an exam for me. I would also write papers and send them directly back to the professor at the university who was running the course.

Both experiences are examples of

The Art of Teaching

what is generally known as "distance education." Wikipedia defines it in the following way:

"Distance education is a mode of delivering education and instruction, often on an individual basis, to students who are not physically present in a traditional setting such as a classroom. Distance learning provides 'access to learning when the source of information and the learners are separated by time and distance, or both.' Distance education courses that require a physical on-site presence for any reason (including taking examinations) have been referred to as hybrid or blended courses of study. Massive open online courses (MOOC), aimed at large-scale interactive participation and open access via the web or other network technologies, are a recent development in distance education."

Here we see a direct connection

being established between distance education and MOOCs. And, despite all hype to the contrary, reason, the rules of definition, and even Wikipedia tell us that MOOCs are simply just a new form of distance education. Let us take a closer look at this definition.

If one really starts to think about all the different activities which can be included in distance education one realizes that a MOOC is not directly a species of the genus "distance education" but rather a species of the genus "online education." This is because "distance education" exists in at least three direct species. These being correspondence, televised, and online courses. And "online education" exists in at least two different species. These being small online courses and massive open online courses.

The Art of Teaching

This is a very important distinction because people who are opposed to MOOCs are often accused of being opposed to online education as a whole (as if MOOCs are the only species of online education). While, in fact, to be against MOOCs is not to be against online education in general, but to be against a certain form of online education. Let us review:

Genus = Distance education.

Species = Correspondence, televised, and online education.

Genus = Online education.

Species = Small online courses, MOOCs.

So just what is the difference between small online courses and massive open online courses? Is there a certain number of students said courses must have in them to be considered "massive" or is some other essential characteristic involved? It is difficult to determine if there is a hard and fast number of students. Some MOOCs have thousands, or even tens of thousands, of students. I would say that the essential characteristic in this regard is not the actual number of students, but the fact that MOOCs are designed to be able to accommodate a massive number of students. Yet just what is the nature of this accommodation? Let us look at this from the student's perspective.

In a MOOC, a great deal of the planning is built into the course, which exists essentially as a computer program, and thus the instructor has limited to no control over it. In a

The Art of Teaching

MOOC, the lectures are taped, and other teaching components pre-packaged. Thus, the student cannot consult directly with the person doing the teaching. In a MOOC, evaluations are often handled by graders, or even other students, whom the individual student has little to no access to and thus can never consult with regarding any grading concerns.

In contrast, in a small online course the student has direct access to the person who plans the course. Thus, if a life event comes up or something in the course plan is simply not practical the student can consult directly with the instructor and adjustments can be made. In a small online course, the student has direct access to the person who teaches the course. Thus, if the material is not being understood or clarifications are needed the student can

The Art of Teaching

consult directly with the instructor. In a small online course, the student has access to the person who evaluates their work. Thus, if some question arises over a grade, or concern over whether an assignment has been counted toward an overall grade, the student can consult directly with the instructor.

The key message here is clear. To be against MOOCs is not to be against online education but to be against impersonal education. To be against MOOCs is to insist that the instructor should be the person who plans, teaches, and evaluates the course and that the student has the right to have access to the instructor in all these various roles.

Certain situations exist where online education is warranted. There are certain students who either cannot

The Art of Teaching

attend or would find great hardship in attending on-campus courses. Many good small online courses have been, and continue to be, taught by dedicated university faculty. The essential difference between these courses and MOOCs is that the instructor has control over pedagogy, teaching, and evaluation, and the students have direct access to the instructor in all these roles.

This is as true of small online courses as it is of on-campus courses, with the exception being that on-campus courses are always preferable because in them the student has direct access not only to the instructor but to his or her classmates and other campus university resources as well.

The Art of Teaching

The Art of Teaching

MOOCS AND ACADEMIC FREEDOM

The Art of Teaching

The Art of Teaching

A LETTER TO A PRO-MOOC STUDENT

Dear Student,

I know a wonderful SJSU professor who teaches every summer and would love to have you in her class. The cost to be taught in person is higher now yet do not be fooled by that. Companies motivated only by profit are lining up to do MOOCs and they will get every cent they can out of you in the end.

I feel your pain as the administration put me in the position of trying to fit 46 students who wanted to add into 6 openings in my class last spring. When all they needed to do to prevent 40 students from being disappointed was to hire another part-time lecturer.

However, this situation goes beyond

The Art of Teaching

mine or your problems. If we start letting Bill Gates decide what courses get taught how long will it be before we start letting Bill Gates decide the content of said courses? (assuming this is not already going on). And once we let people with business profit agendas take over education how long do you think it will be before they start to collect every last cent they can from you?

And what if these businesspeople do not like something you say in class? Do you think you will still be allowed to say it? This is why we have this thing in a public university classroom called Academic Freedom. And it is not just for the instructor but for you, as well! Because of Academic Freedom everyone in class has the right to say whatever they need to say to get at the truth of the subject.

The Art of Teaching

Without this freedom all the progress that has been made on all the issues close to your heart most likely would never have been made because the people in power at the time would never have let anyone speak out. Think about it. What if the oil companies had been running environmental studies?

No Freedom=No Truth=No Progress.

This is why we are fighting against Bill Gates and the other businesspeople who are trying to push MOOCs on us and take over public education. This is what is at stake for everyone--not just you and I. It is important enough to me that I have spoken out openly, possibly putting my job at risk. Yet sometimes we must look beyond our own needs and think of the greater good. I hope once you reflect upon these things you will consider joining us.

The Art of Teaching

The Art of Teaching

A LETTER TO A PRO-MOOC INSTRUCTOR

Dear Professor,

Any professor should know going in that when you give up your control over content and evaluation in teaching a course you have failed already: Failed to be an instructor and become a teaching assistant! There is no need to conduct an experiment any more than there is a need for one to take poison to see if it will make you sick. The only question is how sick and if the patient will ever recover.

This is not to say that distance education in which you maintain control over content and evaluation is bad. Distance education in some circumstances can be a good thing. Particularly when the students have

The Art of Teaching

access to and can get feedback from the instructor. By this I mean the person who plans, teaches, and evaluates the course.

MOOCs simply do not, and more importantly, cannot do these things. This is not to mention the lack of responsibility one shows to their profession, their colleagues, and most importantly, the concept of Academic Freedom by participating in such things. MOOCs were a nice idea originally when they were free and had the pure intention of bringing knowledge to the world. Yet now the power elites have seized upon them and the one thing we can be sure of is that their intentions are not pure.

I think their ultimate intentions are to convert each discipline in higher education into a few MOOCs and then

The Art of Teaching

penetrate the content of said MOOCs. At this point education (teaching people how to think) will become indoctrination (teaching people what to think) aimed at financially benefiting whatever corporate entity is in control of the particular course. Academic Freedom, and the counterbalance it provides against the power elites, will become but a memory. All because some people, who should have known better, did not stand up and fight for it while they still had the chance. I shall not be one of them. Care to join me?[1]

---

[1] Both of these letters were responses to the Chronical of Higher Education article "Inside A MOOC In Progress" by Karen Head on 6/21/2013.

The Art of Teaching

The Art of Teaching

REFUTING THE PRO-MOOC ARGUMENTS

To begin with, the whole discussion of the "cost" issue is really silly. Do any of you know just how much a part-time lecturer gets paid? I have been teaching one course a semester for several years now and my monthly paycheck is $660 after taxes. Even if one were to teach 4-5 courses per semester and reach the top of the pay scale you can maybe make 40K a year. And part-time lecturers are the majority of people teaching at public universities these days. The big universities already have the classrooms in place, so it is just a matter of paying the instructors. So, the whole argument about over-crowded courses is a crisis that has been created by greedy administrators so they can rush to the rescue with "solutions" that will enrich their buddies in high tech!

The Art of Teaching

MOOCs also raise real issues about Academic Freedom. Suppose there get to be 2-3 MOOCs in the whole country that teach intro to psychology. A good course in this would point out that a great deal of depression can be treated with talk therapy (without drugs). What do you think the big pharmaceutical companies will want to do about this inconvenient academic fact? Buy off the 2-3 "star" professors teaching the courses and say that all depression must be treated with drugs. They might even have the audacity to say that depression must be treated only with their brand name drug! This is why we have always put up a "firewall" between big business and academia in this country. MOOCs will reduce that "firewall" to a thin veil.

The Art of Teaching

Doctor Leddy is absolutely right. It is not just university education that is at stake here but, in reality, our entire culture. And who is standing up to guard it? A bunch of brave professors at San Jose State University who I am proud to call my colleagues. As far as I am concerned, they are all worth their weight in gold. [2]

---

[2] This is a comment on the bostonreview.net article "MOOCs: A Threat to Literacy And Bad For Students" by Thomas Leddy on 6/14/2013.

The Art of Teaching

The Art of Teaching

FOLLOW THE MOOC MONEY

So, the SJSU administration has now freely admitted that they are leaving the choice of courses up to Bill Gates. Not only is there not shared governance with their faculty, which is designed to be the norm that protects quality education, but they are not even governing things themselves! So just how much did Bill Gates have to pay to get SJSU to offer the courses he wants? What is the attitude toward Microsoft and other Gates interests put forward in these courses? Wake up you idiots! The SJSU administration has put higher education up for sale to the highest bidder and you are talking about "experiments" and "giving things time" while any sane society would be talking about the arrest of those involved! Oh, what a brave new world we are living in! [3]

[3] From comments on "Udacity Project on 'Pause'" found in

The Art of Teaching

Inside Higher Education on 7/18/2013.

The Art of Teaching

The Art of Teaching

The Art of Teaching

<u>SAN JOSE STATE PROFESSOR HAS BOOK DISPLAYED AT ST. STEPHAN CATHEDRAL IN VIENNA, AUSTRIA.</u>

St. Stephan Cathedral in Vienna, Austria is hosting an interactive art display, and a San Jose State University lecturer has a part in it. *Chromotopia St. Stephan: Via Activa im Dialog des Lichts* by Light artist Victoria Coeln is an interactive display of light and literature currently going on in Vienna's main cathedral.

The "light" is a combination of colored spotlights along with specially colored transparent sheets of film hung inside of the cathedral's windows. Many of the cathedral's original stained-glass windows were destroyed in a 1945 fire and replaced with regular glass. Thus, Coeln's lighting effects seek to

The Art of Teaching

both restore and enhance those of the original stained-glass windows. The "literature" is composed of seven stations spread throughout the interior of the cathedral featuring seven different female authors. In order to make the stations interactive Coeln places books either by or about each author around their respective stations.

Professor John C. Wilhelmsson of the San Jose State University Philosophy Department was recently visiting a friend in Vienna and decided to attend the noon mass. On his way out of the cathedral he happened upon a sign placed on an easel with "Edith Stein" written on it. Curious, he took a closer look and was surprised to find a copy of his recently published book: <u>The Transposition of Edith Stein: Her Contribution to Philosophy, Feminism, and The Theology of the Body</u>

The Art of Teaching

lying beside some of Edith Stein's own works. He said of it:

> *As I looked down, I was both surprised and overjoyed to see, sitting between two of Edith Stein's most important works, my book! It is an honor for my work to be included in a display about Edith Stein but for it to be placed among her works amazed me! I was aware that several copies have been sold in Europe but for me to have come halfway around the world, from San Jose to Vienna, and then see my book in St. Stephan Cathedral brought a great revelatory joy!*

Wilhelmsson sees a greater significance in the event given the current debate over Massive Open Online Courses (MOOCs). Some claim that MOOCs, which use video recorded lectures from privileged private universities to replace real professors, will do more harm than

The Art of Teaching

good to public university students by taking away their direct access to both their professor and classmates. Wilhelmsson goes beyond even this by questioning the very premise that MOOC lectures from Harvard or Stanford are superior to his own.

> *I, for one, am tired of the almost smug assumed superiority present in the debate. In my San Jose State University master's thesis [which is contained in his book] I take on the privileged private university scholars and show them wrong. Their formalistic and, dare I say, "lazy" scholarship is what allowed the minimization of Edith Stein as a philosopher to go on for far too long. And now SJSU President Qayoumi and a bunch of opportunist politicians want to replace a real version of me with a taped version of them! How does this improve education at SJSU? How does*

The Art of Teaching

this increase the prestige of holding an SJSU degree? These are the things I have been working for. Is it too much to ask that the administration might have the same goals?

Yet Wilhelmsson sees an even darker side to the issue than this:

You must ask yourself why a group of power elites are so interested in gaining control of the public university classroom? In our politically correct and increasingly monitored and controlled society, the public university classroom is one of the last great havens where people can speak freely and question authority. MOOCs are more akin to indoctrination, which teaches you what to think, than education, which teaches you how to think. I do not think MOOCs are just bad policy. I think MOOCs are evil.

The Art of Teaching

The *"Chromotopia St. Stephan: Via Activa im Dialog des Lichts"* art display continues until June 8th, 2013.[4]

---

[4] This article was taken from the Chaos to Order Publishing website at WWW.C2OP.COM

The Art of Teaching

The Art of Teaching

The Art of Teaching

MOOC TRUTH.COM

The Art of Teaching

The Art of Teaching

THE ORIGENS OF MOOCTRUTH.COM

Shortly after the MOOC controversy erupted, the San Jose State chapter of the California Faculty Association held a very well attended meeting at a local banquet room. As we considered how to respond to the crisis, I decided to set up a webpage entitled mooctruth.com in order to document the coming events all in one easy to find place.

The first issue was to acquire the webpage address "mooctruth.com" so I could redirect it to a page on education I already had set up on my Chaos to Order Publishing website. This done, I began to gather the important webpage links to articles I would need.

The Art of Teaching

I soon realized that only posting the links with no content at all from the articles was not going to be an effective way to achieve my goal. Then I began creating my own title headings for the links and including some actual linked to article content. This turned out to be a great strategy as some of the links went bad after a time, yet I still had the content which had otherwise been lost to the far places of the internet.

I present mooctruth.com to you now in its current state. I will try to include author names and article titles in the paperback version of this book so you might be able to find many of the linked to articles independently.

The Art of Teaching

Read The SJSU Philosophy Department Open Letter
04/29/2013

"Professors who care about public education should not produce products that will replace professors, dismantle departments and provide a diminished education for students in public universities."

Read It in The New York Times
05/03/2013

"But if we buy them [MOOCs] from edX as the basis for our classes, we would suddenly be second class citizens. I would basically be a teaching assistant, and my students, unlike those at Harvard, could not question their professor."

MOOCs, Shared Governance and

The Art of Teaching

Academic Freedom
05/04/2013

"What does it mean to have a university without professors? CERTAINLY, it makes shared governance the primary means of enforcing quality control upon methods of instruction, a thing of the past. Perhaps more importantly for society at large, what does it mean if future students everywhere get only one view of what justice means? Nobody is censoring anyone if you simply take away their listeners, but on cultural terms that result may be even more disturbing."

-Jonatan Rees

MOOCs A Threat to Literacy and Bad for Students
06/14/2013

"Our concern is… with the future of

The Art of Teaching

higher education itself, and hence, frankly, with the future of our culture. The key problem is not even MOOCs so much as it is with the reduction of knowledge to that which can be tested by a multiple-choice exam. It is the "massive" aspect of MOOCs that raises the deepest problems. MOOCs pose a great threat to the most important value of higher education: "literacy." By "literacy" I mean, very broadly, the ability to read, think about, and intelligently respond (both orally and in writing) to the literature of any field of study. Thus, implementation of MOOCs for university credit is bad because it is bad for our students."

-Thomas Leddy

A Responsible University President Reacts to MOOCs
(dead link).

The Art of Teaching

"Well, with all due respect to Mr, Khan, MIT and Mr. Gates, I very strongly disagree with their implicit assumption about the purpose of education. These new models and their champions take a very narrow and instrumental view of higher education, suggesting that education is primarily, or even exclusively, about improving a student's job market outcomes. These new models of distance and on-line learning do represent new possibilities for some busy adults or young people living in a country without educational opportunities. BUT if I am a smart, motivated high school student, anywhere in the world, the very best holistic education is and will continue to be at a residential liberal arts college. To repeat, I strongly believe that the finest education available in the world for the foreseeable future will be at places like St. John's University and the

The Art of Teaching

College of Saint Benedict. It takes much more than a good internet connection to provide a great education-people and place matter."

Yahoo Meets in Person to Be The "best place to work" Yet Distance Education MOOCs Are OK For University Students. Sounds Like a High-Tech Hypocrisy to Me!
07/10/2013

"To become the absolute best place to work, communication and collaboration will be important, so we need to be working side-by-side. That is why it is critical that we are all present in our offices. Some of the best decisions and insights come from hallway and cafeteria discussions, meeting new people, and impromptu team meetings. Speed and quality are often sacrificed when we work from home. We need to be one Yahoo!, and that starts with physically being together."

-CEO Marissa Mayer

Community College Six See "Unthinking Technophilia"
01/13/2013

"If the unthinking technophilia and new Taylorism which MOOCs represent ends up killing face-to-face education as we know it, it won't be because the technology offers a superior form of education. It will be because our visionless political and educational leaders have almost entirely abandoned educational values for market values. As many scholars have noted, in the era of neoliberalism we have just about given up on the notion of education as a public good rather than a mere commodity. Let's hope we

The Art of Teaching

don't allow this near-total triumph of market values to destroy one of the last public spaces in our society not completely determined by greed and instrumentalism."

What Is the Real Agenda Behind MOOCs?
03/18/2013

"MOOC momentum is being driven not by educational need or proven technological achievement but by a business lobby... The movement's systematic exaggerations, the lack of concern for impacts on public university ecosystem, the staged benevolence toward a hostile customer are all hallmarks not of technical or pedagogical progress, but of a carefully designed business strategy."
                                                         -Chris Newfield

MOOC "Instructor" Realizes That She Is No Longer In Control Of Pedagogy Or Evaluation. That She Has In Effect Become A Teaching Assistant For Coursera

06 20/2013

"My limited ability to make key pedagogical choices is the most frustrating aspect of teaching a MOOC. Because of the way the Coursera platform is constructed, such wide-ranging decisions have been hard-coded into the software—decisions that seem to have no educational rationale and that thwart the intent of our course."

"I wanted to require students to participate in peer work in order to get credit for assignments. When I wanted to make the penalty for not completing peer review a 100-percent deduction per assignment, the Coursera support team responded that the maximum

The Art of Teaching

deduction could be only 20 percent. Coursera acknowledged that other instructors had complained about the penalty figure but gave no indication as to when or whether the problem would be addressed. Predictably, many students have not completed the peer review, leaving others with little feedback. In my opinion, the instructor, not the platform, should determine how an assignment is evaluated."

-Karen Head

The Huge Growth of MOOCs Threatens America's Great Public University System
(dead link)

"You can't teach 200,000 people," she said. "That's just stupid, and that's not how teaching happens. It happens in something called human interaction and through dialogue and conversation.

The Art of Teaching

There are some rock star professors. ... But with 100,000 students, that's no more teaching than a Facebook friendship is a real friendship."

What Is the Real Cost of MOOCs?
04/29/2013

"An article in the Chronicle of Higher Education points out that 'Offering MOOCs through edX is hardly free. There are options available to institutions that want to build their own courses on the edX platform at no charge, but for partners who want help developing their courses, edX charges a base rate of $250,000 per course, then $50,000 for each additional time that course is offered; edX also takes a cut of any revenue the course generates.'"

-Brian Sandberg

Will MOOCs Create Two Classes of

The Art of Teaching

Universities?
(dead link)

"...one with well-funded colleges and universities in which privileged students get their own real professors, and the other consisting of financially stressed private and public universities in which students watch videotaped lectures with some interaction on their home campus."

For Whom Is College Being Reinvented?
12/17/2012

"Read beneath the headlines a bit. The pundits and disrupters, many of whom enjoyed liberal-arts educations at elite colleges, herald a revolution in higher education that is not for people like them or their children, but for others: less-wealthy, less-prepared students who are increasingly cut off

The Art of Teaching

from the dream of a traditional college education."
     -Scott Carlson

The Debate Over MOOCs Reaches Harvard
05/10/2013

 "While the level of unease expressed at Harvard is not as unified or oppositional as recent statements made at American, Duke, and San Jose State Universities, it is all the more notable for arising among the faculty of an institution that has invested $30 million in a nonprofit organization that produces massive open online courses."
     -Anthony Picciano

The Art of Teaching

The Art of Teaching

FAITH, REASON, AND EDUCATION

The Art of Teaching

A TALE OF TWO TRADITIONS

Last weekend I attended two rather interesting events. One was a talk by a Jesuit priest at the Catholic parish where I grew up and the other was a fund raiser for an Islamic high school. Although it was not at all apparent, both events held much deeper connections than just both happening to be a part of my weekend schedule.

These connections date back to the twelfth and thirteenth centuries in the figures of two outstanding scholars. The first is the great Islamic scholar Averroes. Born in Cordoba, Spain in 1126 AD Averroes went on to become one of the greatest thinkers of his day. Highly skilled in law, philosophy, theology, medicine, and many other arts, Averroes was one of the greatest thinkers of all time.

However, ironically, his greatest contributions may have been to Christianity rather than to Islam. This is because Averroes was "The Commentator" on "The Philosopher" himself Aristotle. And these very terms "The Commentator" and "The Philosopher" were coined by none other than the great Catholic scholar Saint Thomas Aquinas. For much of what Aquinas learned about Aristotle in the thirteenth century was due to the commentaries Averroes wrote on him in the twelfth century.

A common theme between these two great thinkers is the relationship between faith and reason. Averroes held that both philosophy and religion were ways to truth—a radical idea in

The Art of Teaching

the Islam of his day. And although Christianity did have an existing tradition of faith and reason Aquinas was forced to defend it against many attacks, ultimately perfecting the idea of the theological syllogism.

A syllogism is a form of argumentation invented by Aristotle. It is composed of several statements, known as premises, which are logically related to one another. For example:

Major premise: All men are mortal.
Minor premise: Socrates is a man.
Conclusion: Socrates is mortal.

In a normal syllogism, the premises can be proven through observation and reason (as indeed is the case here). However, in a theological syllogism, this is sometimes not the case. What Aquinas pointed out, in the famous controversy on the topic at the University of Paris, is that although the premises of a theological syllogism sometimes can't be proven by observation and reason, they can in fact find their proofs in sacred scripture and tradition. Therefore, the new logic of Aristotle can be applied to theology in the form of the theological syllogism!

Thus, a balance in the roles of philosophy and theology was struck in Christianity. And it is a balance which has remained with us until our own day. This is attested to in the encyclical of Pope John Paul II from 1998 entitled "Fides et Ratio" (Faith and Reason). For in it he states:

> *Faith and Reason are like two wings on which the human spirit rises to the contemplation of truth; and God has placed in the human heart a desire to*

The Art of Teaching

> *know the truth—in a word, to know Himself—so that, by knowing and loving God, men and women may also come to the fullness of truth about themselves.*

The beautiful imagery of a bird rising to the contemplation of the truth used by Pope John Paul II here is a clear message that it is only through a balance of faith and reason that a religion can thrive. For what can a bird with only one wing do besides spiral to its demise?

Why is reason so important to faith? Because faith alone, unbalanced by any other force, can become turned in on itself and quite dangerous to those both inside and outside of it. I have seen this in my own life in various versions of both Christianity and Islam. Be it Jonestown or 9/11 we have several recent examples of faith unchecked by reason becoming destructive.

Thus, the struggle to ascend to truth remains for us all. And the brilliance of Averroes high school and the movement behind it is that they have tapped into one of the great figures in the history of this struggle. An Islamic scholar who is also one of the pillars of secular European society because of his insistence that faith must always be guided by reason.

At my Catholic gathering this past weekend unfortunate comments were made. "Professors" were derided for teaching relativism and attacking faith. As a professor of philosophy, I found such comments curious because in just about every philosophy textbook I have seen the refutation of relativism is one of the first orders of business. And in

The Art of Teaching

my own courses it is indeed the first order of business (before we even open the textbook).

In contrast, at the Averroes High School event speakers were lauded for their academic credentials and indeed a non-Islamic professor was the keynote speaker. And, after all was said and done, I had to admit that as an educator I felt somewhat derided at a Catholic event and rather appreciated at a, primarily, Islamic event. And this is not the first time I have encountered a rather anti-academic environment in Christian circles of late. Add to this the recent new translation of the Mass from a clear modern English to an archaic English with Latin grammar and one cannot help but see a trend developing.

It is indeed quite ironic that just as the Catholic faith seems to be forgetting

The Art of Teaching

its great tradition of faith and reason some brave visionaries in the Islamic faith are working to rediscover their own. And this is even more ironic in light of the fact that the works of Averroes were the seed of thought for Aquinas in his great defense of the theological syllogism.

It was indeed an interesting weekend. In fact, a tale of two traditions. A weekend in which I found out that my own tradition has something to learn from another. One in which I came to know about a new movement to combine both faith and reason. And one in which I encountered many hospitable people at both events for whom I am all grateful.

While Averroes High School seems currently to be primarily an Islamic institution, there is certainly a hope,

The Art of Teaching

because of their respect for both faith and reason, that it might one day become an American institution. And perhaps just another example of how immigrants from other lands often serve as the leaven which causes America to once again rise.

The Art of Teaching

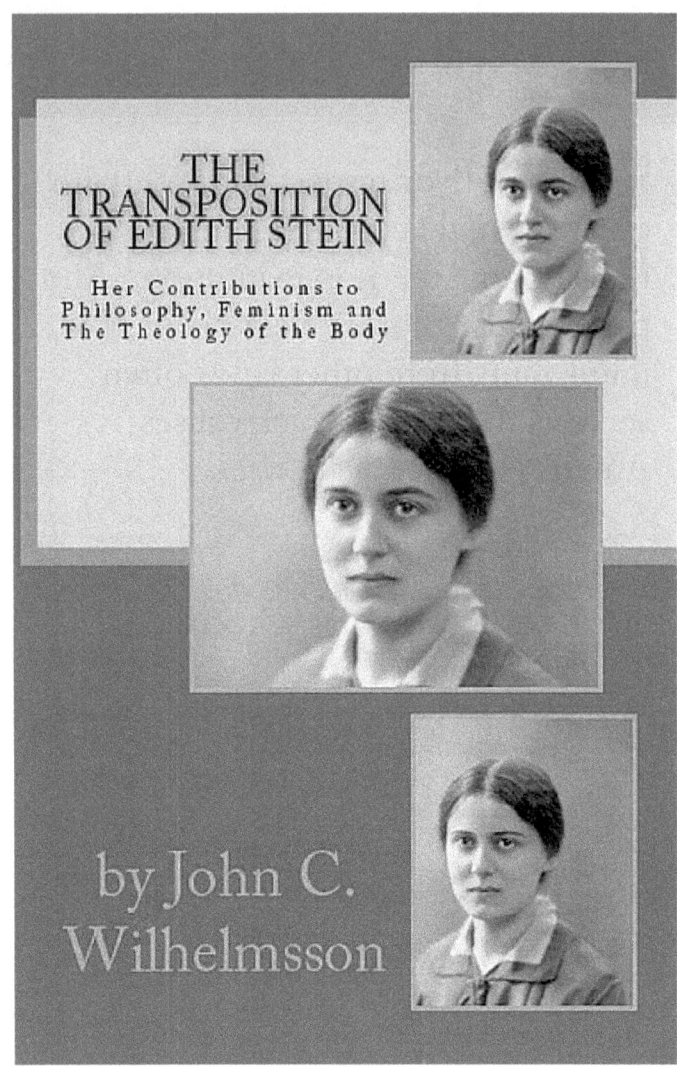

The Art of Teaching

Before she was a Saint, she was a fine philosopher. Yet because she was a woman her contributions were ignored. This book asks the question: "Did Edith Stein make any important contributions to philosophy and, if so, what are the implications of them for us today?" It begins with a biography of Edith Stein up until the acceptance of her doctoral dissertation "On the Problem of Empathy" in 1916. It then examines the phenomenology of Edith Stein and, in new breakthrough research, demonstrates her contributions to twentieth century philosophy as a whole. Finally, it looks at the feminist thought of Edith Stein and its direct connection to "The Theology of the Body" of Pope John Paul II. Here is a book that goes beyond just looking at Stein's thought as a curiosity and instead makes a strong argument for her contributions to philosophy, feminism and "The Theology of the Body."

The Art of Teaching

A Pilgrimage to Iceland

by John Vilhelmsson

The Art of Teaching

After the sudden loss of his father a son recalls a trip they had planned to make together. A trip to his father's homeland of Iceland some fifty years after he had departed. The son decides to set out upon the journey alone in order to honor his father's memory. To set out upon a pilgrimage to Iceland. This true story features many photos. A unique combination of personal, philosophical, and spiritual reflections, this book's sense of immediacy and wonder seeks to bring the reader along on the adventure, while its sense of reverence for the Icelandic culture, land, and people sets it apart from other tales of Iceland. This is Iceland as seen both through the mind and through the heart.

The Art of Teaching

The Art of Teaching

Mary is the most misunderstood figure in the history and current practice of Christianity. This book clarifies her nature and role by looking at four different perspectives. "The personal" tells of our lady of Guadalupe's intercession through the short story "twin fates. "The historical" looks at the origins of the rosary and Mary's influence down through the Christian age. "The scriptural" examines Cardinal Newman's writings on Mary's role purely in terms of sacred scripture. And "the spiritual" details Mary's role as Coredemptrix and the perennial truths of the spiritual life this role points to for us all. Through gathering together all of these perspectives in one book, "Tales of the Theotokos" takes a fresh new look at Mary the mother of Jesus.

The Art of Teaching

The Art of Teaching

Nonni and his younger brother Manni are Icelandic boys who live in the charming town of Akureyri which sits by the Eyjafjörður fjord in northern Iceland. Nonni is curious about many things yet forgetful of his parents' warnings, while Manni is quite innocent and pure of heart and loyal toward Nonni. Thinking he can lure the fish out of the sea with his flute playing Nonni, with trusting Manni at his side, sets out upon the great Eyjafjörður fjord in a small rowboat in order to try. Great adventures follow in this classic and true story of virtue and vocation.

The Art of Teaching

The Art of Teaching

In late 2011 the Catholic mass was changed from the clear modern English of the Novus Ordo mass to an obtuse literal translation from the Latin. According to the theological principle "lex orandi, lex credendi" (as we pray so we believe) this change in the prayer of the Church also brought with it a change in the belief of the Church. Here, through a series of "Faith and Reason" blogs, author John C. Wilhelmsson details the translation change and the effect it is having on Catholic belief. Featuring, "The Old 'We Believe' Crowd," "A Tale of Two Traditions," and the basic ordinary text of the 1973 Novus Ordo mass. Here is a thoughtful reflection on the mass that has shaped the faith of the English speaking Catholic world for the past 40 years, and a vigorous argument why its demise may now hamper the Church's mission in the English speaking world for the next 40 years.

The Art of Teaching

The Art of Teaching

Jon Sveinsson (or "Nonni") is the only Jesuit priest ever born in Iceland. He left his homeland as a boy, with his beloved brother Armann (or "Manni"), to follow their mutual call to become Jesuit missionaries. Although Manni has since passed on during his studies, Nonni is now the Reverend Jon Sveinsson S. J. The boys had wished to become Jesuit missionaries, like St. Francis Xavier, yet Jon Sveinsson has spent most of his time in the order so far as either a student or instructor in academia. Still longing to fulfill his dream of becoming a missionary, he has volunteered to travel to Iceland to care for the souls of his fellow countrymen. And now, after some amount of time, that call is about to be received. Such is the premise of this classic Icelandic travelogue written by the man who would later become one of the most beloved children's authors of all time.

The Art of Teaching

The Art of Teaching

Readings In Classical Ethics fills the need for an ethics reader that is easy to read because it is published in a clear large print. Covering figures from Confucius in the 6th century BC all the way up to Edith Stein in the 20th century AD it is a comprehensive ethics reader. Featuring selections from Western and Eastern philosophy, Christianity, Judaism, and Feminism it is a diverse ethics reader. Published by an ethics instructor at a reasonable price ethics students can afford, "Readings In Classical Ethics" is a great choice for ethics courses or just those with a general interest in the topic.

The Art of Teaching

The Art of Teaching

In an age of conformity brought on by huge cult-like corporations and ubiquitous social media is there still a road less traveled one might choose to follow? How better to confront the conformity of the 21st century than by consulting history's seven great freethinking philosophers? Here in this attractive volume in a clear large print, one can learn how each of these great minds fought against conformity in their own age and learned how to follow their own unique path. And, hopefully, by doing so be enriched and inspired to do the same. Based upon "Half-Hours With The Free Thinkers," yet fully updated with brand new selections on Augustine, Averroes, and Edith Stein, this new version of a classic is a must read for all current, or aspiring, freethinkers.

The Art of Teaching

The Art of Teaching

ABOUT THE AUTHOR

John C. Wilhelmsson is a businessman, professor of philosophy at San Jose State University, best-selling author, and award-winning publisher. After having taught both philosophy and theology he decided to form Chaos to Order Publishing. The goal of which is to create beautiful high-quality books published more for their cultural and spiritual value than for their ability to turn a profit. On 12/12/12 his award-winning San Jose State University master's thesis became the first Chaos to Order Publishing book entitled "The Transposition of Edith Stein: Her Contributions to Philosophy, Feminism, and The Theology of the Body." As both a working philosopher and speaker John is known for his enthusiastic style and thoughtful and independent interpretations.

www.ingramcontent.com/pod-product-compliance
Lightning Source LLC
Chambersburg PA
CBHW071700040426
42446CB00011B/1848